Mark Knight, *Herald Sun*

Andrew Weldon, *The Medical Republic*

Matt Golding, *The Sunday Age*

'We can't hide away, we gotta get through.'
— Dominic Perrottet

'You can choose to wear a mask, you can choose many things to protect your own health. But they're your choices and we have to be careful about imposing our choices on others.'
— Scott Morrison

'There was no planning. We knew there'd be a surge when restrictions were relaxed … They should have maintained the mask mandate, the QR codes, and expanded the testing system.'
— Prof. Raina Macintyre

'Well, people are not dying.'
— Barnaby Joyce

BEST AUSTRALIAN
POLITICAL CARTOONS
2022

Russ Radcliffe created the annual Best Australian Political Cartoons series in 2003. His other books include: *Man of Steel: a cartoon history of the Howard years* in 2007; *Dirt Files: a decade of Australian political cartoons* in 2013; and *My Brilliant Career: Malcolm Turnbull, a political life in cartoons* in 2016.

Russ has edited collections from some of Australia's finest political cartoonists, including Matt Golding, Judy Horacek, Bill Leak, Alan Moir, Bruce Petty, John Spooner, and David Rowe, and curated several exhibitions including Moments of Truth, Dirt Files, and Suppositories of Wisdom.

In 2013 Russ was awarded the Australian Cartoonists Association's Jim Russell Award for his contribution to Australian cartooning.

For my great friend Tony Reid

BEST AUSTRALIAN
POLITICAL CARTOONS
2022

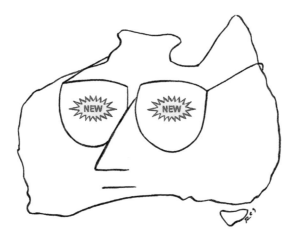

edited by
Russ Radcliffe

SCRIBE

Melbourne • London

Scribe Publications
18–20 Edward St, Brunswick, Victoria 3056, Australia

Published by Scribe 2022

Cover, front: Cathy Wilcox, *The Sydney Morning Herald*
Cover, back: Matt Golding, *The Age*
Title page: Reg Lynch, *The Sydney Morning Herald*

Printed and bound in Australia by Ligare Book Printers

Scribe is committed to the sustainable use of natural resources and the use of paper
products made responsibly from those resources.

Scribe acknowledges Australia's First Nations peoples as the traditional owners and
custodians of this country, and we pay our respects to their elders, past and present.

978 1 922585 46 2

A catalogue record for this book is available from the National Library of Australia.

scribepublications.com.au

cartoonists

David Pope, *The Canberra Times*

'Folly is a more dangerous enemy to the good than evil. You can protest against evil, you can unmask it or prevent it by force. Evil always contains the seeds of its own destruction, for it always makes men uncomfortable, if nothing worse. There is no defense against folly. Neither protests nor force are of any avail against it, and it is never amenable to reason. If facts contradict personal prejudices, there is no need to believe them, and if they are undeniable, they can simply be pushed aside as exceptions. Thus the fool, as compared with the scoundrel, is invariably self-complacent. And he can easily become dangerous, for it does not take much to make him aggressive. Hence folly requires much more cautious handling than evil.'
— Dietrich Bonhoeffer

'In individuals, insanity is rare; but in groups, parties, nations, and epochs, it is the rule.'
— Friedrich Nietzsche

introduction

The year 2022 began with optimism — the worst of the pandemic seemed to be over, and a return to a level of normality was imminent. After a remarkably stoic communal response to the long and grinding COVID lockdowns in New South Wales and Victoria, the widespread take-up of COVID vaccines allowed divergent state strategies to be dialled back, and the centrifugal forces flinging the nation apart stilled (p. 6). Australia was once again a unified country.

Even as the more draconian measures, with all their attendant mental and economic pain, were being wound back, frustration and tensions were boiling over — with a little help from an anti-vax Pauline Hanson and some of the more 'liberationist' elements on the right, such as George Christensen and Craig Kelly (p. 14). The mantras of pushing through, personal responsibility, and choice became the official rhetoric — strategies that, for a still apprehensive population, might have been a little easier to bear had the lackadaisical attitude to vaccines procurement not been repeated with rapid antigen tests.

Clearly, high vaccination rates were remarkably successful and liberating, but the uncontrolled spread of Omicron inevitably resulted in a rapid increase in COVID deaths. After years of obsessive number-watching at daily briefings, the continuing high infection rates are now out of sight and out of mind (p. 150).

With the nation spared bushfires, at least, this year, it was the turn of Australia's other natural charm — flooding rains — to provide the annual once-in-a-century climate disaster to stress-test our national resilience, destroying lives and livelihoods in the process (p. 68). Even the Coalition grudgingly acknowledged the anthropomorphic role in the foreseen 'cascading and compounding' impacts we are now witnessing. But the internal warfare within the Coalition inevitably came to the fore in the debate over net zero targets preceding COP 26 in Glasgow (p. 60). The loudest voices came from the usual suspects — Liberal and National — threatening to blow up yet another government; they were still more than a match after a decade of such behaviour for the pusillanimous Liberal moderates. The so-called Australian way provided the rhetorical compromise, and was widely viewed as little more than the self-interested prevarications of fossil-fuel apologists (p. 52).

Internationally, the brutal yet incompetent Russian invasion of Ukraine brought the spectre of war back to Europe, triggering an extraordinary national fightback lead by an unlikely but inspirational president. A parliamentary Zoom session or photo op with Vlodymyr Zelenskyy became de rigueur for Western politicians, especially of the faux Churchillian variety, keen to bask in the glow of the camo-clad charisma of a genuine wartime leader.

Putin's grounds for the invasion were based on the imperial assumption that Ukraine rightfully belonged to greater Russia, it's separate identity a fiction, and the possibility of its joining an

Reg Lynch, *The Sydney Morning Herald*

Matt Golding, *The Age*

expansionist NATO an existential threat — a Russian red line that many sober Western observers have warned about for decades. Clearly, his strategy has severely backfired: the Ukrainian sense of national identity has intensified under his attack, while an enlarged NATO is congratulating itself on a reinvigorated sense of purpose.

Of course, the Ukraine invasion invited comparisons to problems in our own backyard. There was lots of loud and loose talk about an 'arc of autocracy' and of a new cold war with Russia and China — as if the ghost of the first cold war was the only possible frame of reference for understanding the relationship between competing powers (p. 38).

The Coalition government signalled that its long-term strategy for managing our relationship with China was getting the boys in the Anglosphere back together (p. 28). The French would just get over the cancellation of the submarine contract, and our South-East Asian neighbours alarmed at such an escalation … well, *C'est la vie*. Nuclear submarines — designed to link in with US strategic requirements — remove any room for independent manoeuvre and, in effect, simply shrug off the idea that our national interests might differ from the US for decades to come. It is a foreign policy of wishful thinking, ignoring the possibility that a Trump, or worse, might not only be a fickle and capricious ally, but may well be the belligerent in any conflict. Alternatively, there is a real possibility that the US may simply retreat from a region it concludes is not worth the effort to dominate. Nevertheless, it's all the way with …

It was, at times, hard to regard the Coalition as a government serious about anything apart from its own survival. Nowhere was this lack of gravitas revealed more clearly than in foreign policy. Even the hard-nosed pros at ASIO castigated Morrison and Dutton for their shouty bellicosity and transparently political accusations about Labor's appeasement of China — designed, of course, to set up a national security election, regardless of the international consequences (p. 32). Still, apart from minor rhetorical variations, there was no substantive policy debate between the major parties about these most significant of relationships: about why we should even consider prosecuting a war with China, never mind how, and certainly no truthful accounting of the likely impact on the nation or the price in Australian blood of another major Asian war. Nada.

The international environment was bad enough, but then we had the grinding tedium of a six-week ideas-free election campaign between a clamorous but intellectually torpid incumbent and a risk-averse opposition suffering a form of electoral PTSD and desperate to atone for the 2019 election loss (p. 100).

As well as Morrison's deep personal unpopularity and distrust, the Coalition's perceived failures were legion and electorally very costly (p. 92). The provision of vaccines and RATS — the route to pandemic salvation — should have been seen as a triumph of effective government. Instead, they became bywords for incompetence, and proof that Morrison's government couldn't handle basic and essential public administration. The failures of aged-care provision cemented that view.

With its reputation for dodgy dealings and looking after its mates, the Coalition remained implacably resistant to all attempts at establishing institutional protections for integrity in government. As well as its customary climate obstructionism, the Coalition failed to address the small matter of the nation's long-term energy security. Timing was damaging for the Coalition in a number of critical areas. The announcement of the Chinese deal in the Solomon Islands killed the Coalition's hairy-chested national security credentials and any possibility of a scary khaki election (p. 114). And an interest-rate rise, due more to international conditions than domestic policy, nevertheless damaged the central claim to fame of all Coalition governments — that they could manage the economy better than the spendthrift left (p. 116).

The most egregious aspects of Morrison's cultural dog-whistle techniques were on display with his support of Catherine Deves in New South Wales, and his politicisation of an issue peripheral to most but intensely cruel to some (p. 122). The Canberra bubble, where adults ran things with calm efficiency, and decent, quiet Australians left them to it, was shown to be not just another half-baked Morrisonism, but a strategy to efface the real and vital contestation in politics — especially the troublesome woke variety that he couldn't stomach. Take a bow, Brittany Higgins and Grace Tame (p. 78).

While Clive Palmer's liberation yellow might have been evident at most voting booths, it was the colour teal and a bunch of smart, thoughtful women who emerged from Liberal heartlands demanding integrity in government and action on climate that most freaked out the Coalition (p. 124). It turns out that some people were paying attention, after all.

Having spent the previous three years desperately trying not to differentiate themselves from the Coalition, it was unsurprising that Labor's election campaign was vapid and uninspiring. But Albanese came into his own on election night with a passionate and authentically Labor victory speech that left everyone wondering why he hadn't delivered it during the campaign. Despite the Coalition's attempt to brand him as inexperienced, Albanese entered parliament in 1995 and knows intimately how it works. And he has an experienced team hungry to govern and desperate to put previous disasters behind them.

The energy of the first few months was in stark contrast to the previous incumbents. This was nowhere more apparent than in foreign policy. While their stated policies weren't so different, their tone clearly was. Albanese and Penny Wong's post-election trips — to the Pacific Forum, the Quad in Japan, NATO in Europe, South-East Asia, and Wong's Malaysian hometown return — were aimed at resuscitating Australia's good name in the region (p. 170). The Chinese reaction to Nancy Pelosi's Taiwan trip demonstrated just how tenuous is our security in the world in which we now live (p. 176). Managing our regional relationships will be a formidable task.

Massive public debt, the return with a vengeance of inflation, and stagnant wage growth present economic challenges not seen for decades (p. 138). It's a cliche of incoming governments to discover undisclosed budget black holes that require them to rescind election promises. But, haunted by the memory of Abbott's attacks on Gillard's supposed carbon tax backflip, Labor are desperate to demonstrate their trustworthiness and to not provide ammunition to a rampaging Dutton. Labor's me-too approach on the stage-three tax cuts in opposition has deprived them of significant room to manoeuvre (p. 146). The passage of Labor's climate bill with the help of the teals, while small in

Matt Golding, *The Age*

ambition, seemed like a significant achievement — at least a very late start — after ten years of climate recalcitrance (p. 160).

In the end, Morrison's greatest achievement, after the 'miracle' of 2019, was becoming the first prime minister to serve a full term since John Howard. But he left the Coalition a smoking ruin, with only 58 seats in the House of Representatives, the Liberal centre hollowed out, and their bluest-ribbon seats lost (p. 128). Revelations about his secret shadowing of Cabinet positions confirmed the feelings of intense distrust and ill-will towards him from his own side, further diminishing his stature and legacy (p. 136). Morrison may not have quite been a Trump or a Johnson, but it wasn't for want of trying. And, given his scant regard for long-standing political conventions, he looks at home in Pope's diner of discarded populists (p. vi).

Morrison's demise ended nine years of Coalition government inaugurated by Tony Abbott. It ended, in many ways, how it began — at war with itself, warmists, women, and the woke. It was a decade of governments that rarely transcended Abbott's initial reactionary impulses — too ill-prepared and banal in their thinking to have any genuine policy ambitions. With the exception of Turnbull's disastrous attempt to put the 'l' back in Liberalism, they left the impression of unimaginative, self-absorbed governments more concerned with acquiring than exercising power. Oh, hang on — there were tax cuts.

Many people have felt a new sense of possibility in 2022: out with the tired, negligent, and knackered, and in with the energetic, efficient, and responsible. Early days! Things certainly feel a little different in the domestic arena. But the natural catastrophes of recent years — fire, flood, and plague — have, or should have, reminded us that our human position in the great chain of being on Earth is highly contingent. And now war and rumours of war abound. The invasion of Ukraine and the increasingly reckless antagonisms in the western Pacific remind us that empires come and go, but that the great games of global power politics are alive and well. We will live under their shadow for years to come.

— Russ Radcliffe

David Rowe, *Australian Financial Review*

'It has been quite a few years, hasn't it? These last three years. Floods. Fires. Drought. Pandemic. Mouse plague. I turned to Josh Frydenberg one day in Cabinet, I said, I think it's time we let your people go, Josh.'
— Scott Morrison

'Why would you do this job if you don't want to leave a legacy and change Australia for the better?'
— Anthony Albanese

'It is the closest thing to magic in politics: how an election like the last one, in a beat, flips the world upside down. It's as if someone has changed the channel, or the lens, or turned it back to front. The familiar goes suddenly out of focus and retreats, the real becomes unreal, words prove seasonable.'
— Don Watson

let 'er rip

Glen Le Lievre, www.lelievrecartoons.com

'We have no choice but to ride the wave. What's the alternative? What we must do is press on.'
— Scott Morrison

'[Use] personal responsibility and common sense and be cautious over the Christmas break.'
— Dominic Perrottet

'Perrottet, the Boy Blunder on work experience as premier, figures out playing Russian roulette between libertarian ideology and people's lives might just backfire.'
— Kevin Rudd

Andrew Dyson, *The Age*

Glen Le Lievre, www.lelievrecartoons.com

Cathy Wilcox, *The Sydney Morning Herald*

Sean Leahy, *The Courier Mail*

Christopher Downes, *The Mercury*

Dean Alston, *The West Australian*

Matt Golding, *The Sunday Age*

'We're at a stage of the pandemic where you can't just go around making everything free.'
— Scott Morrison

'We've now begun to heavily rely on antigen testing ... access to those tests really has to be free.'
— Prof. Sharon Lewin

'If a rapid test was a rort in a marginal seat, Scott Morrison would be into it like a rat up a drainpipe.'
— Jim Chalmers

'We all knew that once we opened up ... elimination tests would be an important part of the response to keep people safe, and the government simply didn't do anything about it.'
— Anthony Albanese

Jon Kudelka, *The Saturday Paper*

John Farmer, *The Mercury*

David Pope, *The Canberra Times*

'The totalitarian regimes responsible for the most heinous atrocities in the 20th century — think Stalin, Mao, Hitler, Pol Pot — they didn't get there overnight ... state premiers are racing down that familiar path ... The totalitarian path, the path that we are unquestionably on, has never ended well. The solution is a rediscovery of human dignity along with, and I don't say this lightly, civil disobedience.'
— George Christensen

'We don't live in a free society, we live in a prison camp.'
— Craig Kelly

'I think Australians have had a gutful of governments telling them what to do in their lives.'
— Scott Morrison

'It will be a lot better when he stops double speaking to extremists.'
— Dan Andrews

David Rowe, *Australian Financial Review*

Christopher Downes, *The Mercury*

Glen Le Lievre, www.lelievrecartoons.com

'I'm not putting something in my body that doctors tell me there is shit in it ... I have no intentions on listening to these bureaucrats and academics, they are not true scientists.'
 — Pauline Hanson

'It's time for governments to step back and for Australians to take their lives back.'
 — Scott Morrison

'Labor is the enemy of the free people of Australia.'
 — Matt Canavan

'This prime minister has done nothing to prevent this pandemic of discrimination.'
 — Pauline Hanson

'Being held accountable for your own actions isn't called discrimination — it is called being a bloody adult ... You have the freedom to make a choice, but those choices have consequences.'
 — Jacqui Lambie

Matt Bissett-Johnson, *Rationale Magazine*

Warren Brown, *The Daily Telegraph*

rules are rules

Glen Le Lievre, www.lelievrecartoons.com

'Rules are rules, especially when it comes to our borders.'
 — Scott Morrison

'Novak Djokovic may be held for nine hours or nine days. But we have been medically abused ... We are discriminated against because we came by boat, not plane. There was no caring. We came for safety, not to play tennis. It's not sporting or fair. Please, we want our freedom.'
 — Park Hotel refugee

'I am very much aware of a lot of the commentary that is happening but my job as Australia's Home Affairs Minister is to protect our borders.'
 — Karen Andrews

Andrew Dyson, *The Age*

Cathy Wilcox, *The Sydney Morning Herald*

Glen Le Lievre, www.lelievrecartoons.com

'It's been a complete trauma. We came as children, we were boys, and we never had a childhood, we were just put in a cage. We did not receive a proper education, we were never allowed to have fun, we just had to try to survive.'
— Mehdi Ali

'There is no protection owed. They have not been found to be refugees. And so Australia's rules do not permit permanent visas for people who have not been found to be refugees. That is the government's policy.'
— Scott Morrison

'We are a strong enough society to say that we should not treat people badly, in order to send a message to others. It's beyond my comprehension how this has gone on for so long, at enormous cost.'
— Anthony Albanese

Fiona Katauskas, *The Echidna*

Jon Kudelka, *The Saturday Paper*

can-do capitalism

Matt Golding, *The Sunday Age*

'"Can-do capitalism", not "don't-do governments" … We've got a bit used to governments telling us what to do over the last couple of years. I think we have to break that habit.'
— Scott Morrison

'We understand, just as Menzies did, that the foundation for a strong economy rests on individual aspiration, reward for effort and free enterprise. As we emerge from this crisis, we embrace these principles and now have an opportunity not seen for decades to drive down unemployment even further.'
— Josh Frydenberg

'They want to legislate everything. They don't trust Australians to just get on and do it.'
— Scott Morrison

**First Dog
on the Moon**,
The Guardian

Alan Moir, www.moir.com.au

'Tonight, as we gather, war rages in Europe. The global pandemic is not over. Devastating floods have battered our communities. We live in uncertain times. The last two years have been tough for our country, there have been setbacks along the way. But Australia remains resilient. Australians remain strong. We have overcome the biggest economic shock since the Great Depression. Our recovery leads the world.'
   — Josh Frydenberg

'This has all the sincerity of a fake tan. This is a plan for an election, not a plan for Australia's future.'
   — Anthony Albanese

'We've got to give Australians a shield against these cost-of-living pressures that could frustrate and break up the momentum of the economy.'
   — Scott Morrison

'Is it pensions? Is it Medicare? Is it something else? We shouldn't be going to the election with those secret cuts in the budget that will only be unleashed on the Australian people if the Coalition is returned.'
   — Jim Chalmers

Cathy Wilcox, *The Sydney Morning Herald*

Dean Alston, *The West Australian*

Andrew Weldon, *The Big Issue*

'The best way to support people renting a house is to help them buy a house.'
— Scott Morrison

'Thirty per cent of low income people on the private rental market do not have $500 in savings for emergencies, let alone a 5 per cent deposit for a home loan.'
— Chris Martin

'People who are buying houses are renters. And ensuring that more renters can buy their own home and get the security of home ownership, this is one of the key focuses of this Budget.'
— Scott Morrison

'The housing measures announced in last night's budget will only push up house prices. They won't help people on the lowest incomes keep a roof over their head.'
— Cassandra Goldie

Fiona Katauskas, *The Echidna*

Christopher Downes, *The Mercury*

the nuclear option

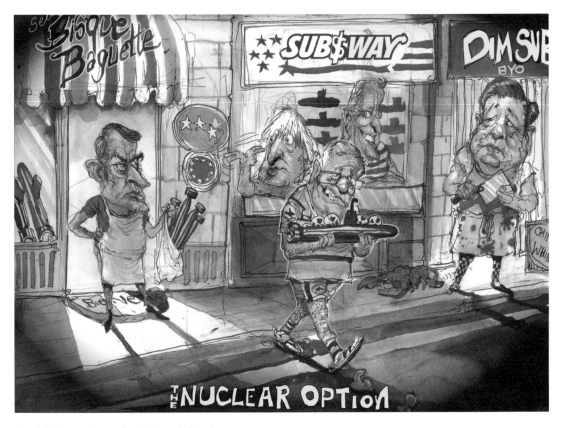

David Rowe, *Australian Financial Review*

'I don't think, I know.'
— Emmanuel Macron

'I think what happened was … clumsy. It was not done with a lot of grace.'
— Joe Biden

'It was a contract. We didn't steal an island. We didn't deface the Eiffel Tower.'
— Barnaby Joyce

Peter Broelman, www.broelman.com.au

Andrew Weldon, *The Big Issue*

Matt Golding, *The Sunday Age*

'I describe [it] as a forever partnership ... for a new time between the oldest and most trusted of friends.'
— Scott Morrison

'It's obvious the real policy is to subsidise the US Navy's submarine budget ... they're essentially US boats operated in the US's great power interests.
— Clinton Fernandes

'He has sacrificed Australian honor, security, and sovereignty.'
— Malcolm Turnbull

'At Morrison's instigation, Australia turns its back on the 21st century, the century of Asia, for the jaded and faded Anglosphere — the domain of the Atlantic — a world away.'
— Paul Keating

Mark Knight, *Herald Sun*

Warren Brown, *The Daily Telegraph*

David Rowe, *Australian Financial Review*

'A new arc of autocracy is instinctively aligning to challenge and reset the world order in their own image.'
— Scott Morrison

'Some people want to pretend it's not a reality in our lifetime ... that was the attitude of the 1930s. We've got to learn the lessons of history and make sure they're not repeated.'
— Peter Dutton

'We urge the Australian side to abandon the outdated Cold War zero-sum mentality and narrow-minded geopolitical perception, handle its relationship with China in a genuinely independent manner, stop sliding further down on the road of harming China–Australia relations.'
— Chinese embassy

THE DRUMS OF WAR...

Alan Moir, www.moir.com.au

Brett Lethbridge, *The Courier Mail*

David Pope, *The Canberra Times*

'We now see evidence, Mr Speaker, that the Chinese Communist Party, the Chinese government, has also made a decision about who they're going to back in the next federal election, Mr Speaker, and that is open and that is obvious, and they have picked this bloke as that candidate.'
— Peter Dutton

'I'll leave the politics to the politicians, but I'm very clear with everyone that I need to be that that's not helpful for us.'
— Mike Burgess, ASIO

'They will not find a fellow traveller when it comes to threats and coercion against Australia in my government, Mr Speaker.'
— Scott Morrison

'On an issue as central as China, it is clearly in the national interest for there to be a bipartisan approach.'
— Denis Richardson

Jim Pavlidis, *The Age*

Jon Kudelka, *The Saturday Paper*

I need ammunition, not a ride

Dean Alston, *The West Australian*

Mark Knight, *Herald Sun*

David Rowe, *Australian Financial Review*

'Ukraine never had a tradition of genuine statehood … they began to build their statehood on the denial of everything that unites us.'
— Vladimir Putin

'This night will be very difficult … the fate of Ukraine is being decided right now.'
— Volodymyr Zelenskyy

'Russian warship … go fuck yourself.'
— Ukrainian soldier, Snake Island

'Everything indicated that a clash with the neo-Nazis … backed by the United States … was inevitable.'
— Vladimir Putin

Badiucao, @badiucao

'China and Russia's cooperation has no forbidden areas, but it has a bottom line ... That line is the tenets and principles of the UN Charter, the recognised basic norms of international law and international relations ... Had China known about the imminent crisis, we would have tried our best to prevent it.'
— Qin Gang

'The Taiwan question and the Ukraine issue are fundamentally different. To compare those two is absurd. We once again urge the US to abide by the One China principle.'
— Wang Wenbink

'Russia is ready to strengthen multilateral coordination with China so as to make constructive efforts in boosting multipolarisation of the world, and establishing a more just and reasonable international order.'
— Xi Jinping, Xinhua report

Andrew Dyson, *The Age*

Mark Knight, *Herald Sun*

Badiucao, @badiucao

'I need ammunition, not a ride.'
  — Volodymyr Zelenskyy

'Take those seeds and put them in your pocket, at least sunflowers will grow when you all lie down here.'
  — Ukrainian woman to Russian solider

'How can I be a Nazi? Explain it to my grandfather, who went through the entire war in the infantry of
  the Soviet army, and died a colonel in an independent Ukraine.'
  — Volodymyr Zelenskyy

'There is no purgatory for war criminals. They go straight to hell, ambassador.'
  — Ukrainian ambassador to Russian ambassador

'When you attack us, you will see our faces, not our backs.'
  — Volodymyr Zelenskyy

Dean Alston, *The West Australian*

Cathy Wilcox, *The Sydney Morning Herald*

David Rowe, *Australian Financial Review*

'If Ukraine was to join NATO it would serve as a direct threat to the security of Russia ... they try to convince us over and over again that NATO is a peace-loving and purely defensive alliance, saying that there are no threats to Russia ... But we know the real value of such words.'
— Vladimir Putin

'We want to see Russia weakened to the degree that it can't do the kinds of things that it has done in invading Ukraine.'
— Lloyd Austin

'Being the arsenal of democracy also means good-paying jobs for American workers in Alabama, in the states all across America, where defense equipment is manufactured and assembled.'
— Joe Biden

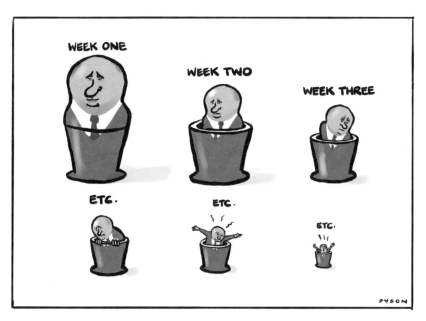

Andrew Dyson, *The Age*

Andrew Dyson, *The Age*

David Pope, *The Canberra Times*

'In more than two and a half years of conversations with key Russian players, from knuckle-draggers in the dark recesses of the Kremlin to Putin's sharpest liberal critics, I have yet to find anyone who views Ukraine in NATO as anything other than a direct challenge to Russian interests.'
— William J. Burns, USA ambassador to Moscow, 2008

'If you believe that the final outcome of your effort has to be the imposition of your values, then I think equilibrium is not possible.'
—Henry Kissinger

'The result is an absence of checks and balances in Russia, and the decision of one man to launch a wholly unjustified and brutal invasion of Iraq — I mean of Ukraine ... Iraq, too. Anyway ...'
— President George W. Bush

'The United States and Israel ... firmly reject the BDS campaign.'
— US–Israel Strategic Partnership Joint Declaration

Andrew Weldon, *The Big Issue*

Andrew Dyson, *The Age*

John Spooner, *The Australian*

'Mariupol. The Apocalypse District. Should we show it to the entire world? Yes. Let Kiev, Lvov, Poltava, Ternopol see: if a city doesn't surrender, it will be destroyed.'
— All-Russian TV and Radio Broadcasting Company

'We should not talk about half measures. Today, all the red lines are crossed. Thousands of peaceful citizens have been killed. Bucha has been obliterated, fucking obliterated. And you think we're going to agree to half measures?'
—Ivan Fedorov, mayor of Melitopol

'Any people, and especially the Russian people, will always be able to distinguish the true patriots from the scum and the traitors, and just to spit them out like a midge that accidentally flew into their mouth ... I am convinced that this natural and necessary self-cleansing of society will only strengthen our country, our solidarity, cohesion, and readiness to meet any challenge.'
— Vladimir Putin

Alan Moir, www.moir.com.au

John Farmer, *The Mercury*

David Pope, *The Canberra Times*

'None of you can feel safe when there is a war in Ukraine, when there is a war in Europe.'
— Volodymyr Zelenskyy

'And I know that it's the instinct of the people of this country, like the people of Ukraine, to choose freedom, every time ... When the British people voted for Brexit ... It's because they wanted to be free.'
— Boris Johnson

'They have only one objective: to prevent the development of Russia. They are going to do it in the same way as they did it before, without furnishing even a single pretext, doing it just because we exist.'
— Vladimir Putin

'The United States and Israel affirm that they will continue to work together to combat all efforts to boycott or de-legitimise Israel, to deny its right to self-defense, or to unfairly single it out in any forum, including at the United Nations or the International Criminal Court.'
— US–Israel Strategic Partnership Joint Declaration

David Pope, *The Canberra Times*

Alan Moir, www.moir.com.au

Brett Lethbridge, *The Courier Mail*

David Pope, *The Canberra Times*

Brett Lethbridge, *The Courier Mail*

'They are trying to blackmail us again … a pretext for a sanctions attack will always be found or fabricated, regardless of the situation in Ukraine. There is only one goal — to restrain the development of Russia.'
  — Vladimir Putin

'He's essentially weaponised hunger … among the poorest people around the world. What we cannot have is any lifting of sanctions, any appeasement, which will simply make Putin stronger in the longer term.'
  — Liz Truss

'This food crisis is real, and we must find solutions.'
  — Ngozi Okonjo-Iweala, World Trade Organization

'Sanctions, restrictions on Russia cause much more damage to those countries that impose them … Further use of sanctions may lead to even more severe — without exaggeration, even catastrophic — consequences on the global energy market.'
  — Vladimir Putin

the Australian way

David Pope, *The Canberra Times*

'Under our plan ... we can make our own Australian way.'
— Scott Morrison

'We have a real plan to deliver on our commitments, one that relies on technology not taxes.'
— Angus Taylor

'We believe climate change will ultimately be solved by "can-do" capitalism; not "don't-do" governments seeking to control people's lives ... with interventionist regulation and taxes.'
— Scott Morrison

'There is net zero modelling, net zero legislation and net zero unity ... As always, with this prime minister, it is all about marketing. All about the spend, never about the substance.'
— Anthony Albanese

John Farmer, *The Mercury*

John Farmer, *The Mercury*

Andrew Weldon,
The Big Issue

John Shakespeare,
The Sydney Morning Herald

David Rowe, *Australian Financial Review*

'This is not a pantomime, we're not grandstanding, we're not trying to prevaricate but we are going to be diligent.'
— Barnaby Joyce

'Last week the minister told question time, "Find me a solar panel that works in the dark". Is the minister aware that batteries can store renewable energy? Does the minister get a shock when he turns on the tap and water comes out even though it is not raining outside?'
— Anthony Albanese

'We don't need hydrogen. Hydrogen hubs are not going to defend us against military bases in the Solomon Islands. We need reliable power now. And that's why we should be building coal-fired power stations.'
— Matt Canavan

Cathy Wilcox, *The Sydney Morning Herald*

Jon Kudelka,*The Saturday Paper*

David Pope, *The Canberra Times*

'Legislation brings in laws, and laws outlaw things, and laws enforce penalties, so we do have a clear differentiation, we have a chasm between the two different policies because we believe in inspiration and technology and they believe in laws and penalties.'
— Barnaby Joyce

'The modelling shows that a clear focus on driving down technology costs will enable Australia to achieve net zero emissions by 2050 without putting industries, regions, or jobs at risk.'
— Angus Taylor

'Scott Morrison's climate ambition is so low that he doesn't even hit net zero in his net zero plan.'
— Adam Bandt

'The future of this crucial industry will be decided by the Australian government, not a foreign body that wants to shut it down, costing thousands of jobs and billions of export dollars for our economy.'
— Keith Pitt

Matt Golding, *The Sunday Age*

Glen Le Lievre, www.lelievrecartoons.com

David Rowe, *Australian Financial Review*

'A growing number of G20 developed economies have announced meaningful emissions reductions by 2030 ... with a handful of holdouts, such as Australia.'
— António Guterres

'The chattering classes of the UN can say what they want ... we're getting on with delivering outcomes.'
— Paul Fletcher

'Australia is just not stepping up and nobody is buying Australia's bullshit anymore.'
— Kavita Naidu

'The Australia Pavilion has the best coffee — it's the least they could do.'
— overheard at COP

John Farmer, *The Mercury*

Mark Knight, *Herald Sun*

Scott doubles down on climate

Mark David, independentaustralia.net

Fiona Katauskas, *The Echidna*

UN CLIMATE
CHANGE
CONFERENCE
AUS 2056

WELCOME DELEGATES TO BROKEN HILL
Host city of the 2056 UN Climate Change Conference

AUSTRALIA

Why Broken Hill? The "Hill" was chosen because of its spectacular NEW location on Australia's Pacific east coast and offers delegates freedom of movement within the safety of its Green-Nuclear™ biome.

"Let's UN-Broken the World!"

Save the world, in safety
COP56 promises the safety of a fortified security state that vigorously maintains a zero-tolerance approach to environmental dissent. Similarly, Broken Hill is now one of only five certified Refugees-Removed™ metropolises in the world.

COP56 IS NOT ALL "BLAH BLAH BLAH"
Australia is the world leader in awesome eco-adventures!

Visit the deepest coal pit in the world

Explore the functioning uranium mines outside the perimeter in our Supa-Safe Bio-Bags™

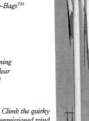

Pat real-life animatronics of recently extinct fauna, including the silver gull, black rat, feral pigeon and koala

Witness the signing of a NEW nuclear submarine deal

Climb the quirky decommissioned wind turbine towers

SCUBA dive around Australia's last functioning desalination plant

Try your hand at extinguishing a raging firestorm. We bet you can't!

KEYNOTE SPEECH
Prime Minister Scott Morrison

In a speech titled "I Will Burn For You!", Australia's longest serving PM (age 88) will address the topic of controlled climate change and God's providential plan for getting to net zero by 2090.

PLEASE NOTE
COP56 is unable to source seafood, meat products, clean water, contaminant-free vegetables or particle-free oxygen.

COP56 says *thank you* to the following organisations, without which this climate conference would not be necessary:

StarGases

China Plate Petroleum

The Fossils Group

AusNuke

Apocalypse

Apocalypse Holdings

Oslo Davis, *The Monthly*

Cathy Wilcox, *The Sydney Morning Herald*

'We Pacific nations have not travelled to the other end of the world to watch our future be sacrificed at the altar of appeasement of the world's worst emitters.'
— Voreqe Bainimarama, Fiji's prime minister

'What was so disappointing for us is the way it appeared your prime minister really doesn't understand the urgency of what we have to do ... Nations around you will disappear beneath the sea because that's what is going to happen to the South Pacific.'
— Lord Deben, UK's Climate Change Committee

'Sounds like his lordship's got plenty of advice for the colonies. Well I've got some advice for his lordship. We need to stick to the facts.'
— Keith Pitt

'The other thing to say is the net zero thing is all sort of dead anyway ... Boris Johnson said he is pausing the net zero commitment, Germany is building coal and gas infrastructure, Italy's reopening coal-fired power plants. It's all over. It's all over bar the shouting here.'
— Matt Canavan

David Pope, *The Canberra Times*

Megan Herbert, *The Age*

First Dog on the Moon, *The Guardian*

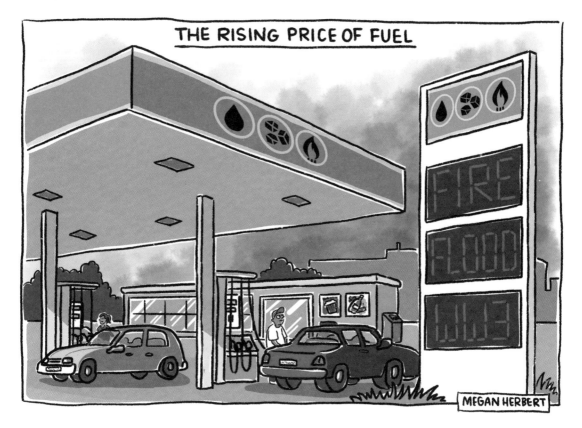

Megan Herbert, *The Age*

'In 2020–21, Australian federal and state governments provided a total of $10.3 billion worth of spending and tax breaks to assist fossil fuel industries. The $7.8 billion cost of the fuel tax rebate alone is more than the budget of the Australian Army. Over the longer term, $8.3 billion is committed to subsidising gas extraction, coal-fired power, coal railways, ports, carbon capture and storage, and other measures.'
— Australia Institute

'Humanity does not lack the resources, technology, projects, innovative potential to achieve it — all that is missing, ladies and gentlemen, is the courage to act.'
— Voreqe Bainimarama

'And if they're buying, we're selling. If we aren't filling that market, somebody else will.'
— Keith Pitt

cascading and compounding

Reg Lynch,
The Sun Herald

Mark David,
independentaustralia.net

Jon Kudelka, *The Saturday Paper*

'Climatic trends, extreme conditions, and sea level rise are already hitting many of Australia's ecosystems, industries, and cities hard. As climate change intensifies, we are now seeing cascading and compounding impacts and risks, including where extreme events coincide ... While the work of adaptation has begun, we have found the progress is uneven and insufficient, given the risks we face.'
 — IPCC, March 2022

'Scott Morrison has been a cigarette salesman in a cancer ward at this conference. The whole world is saying we need to get out of coal and gas ... and Scott Morrison is giving them the middle finger.'
 — Adam Bandt

'They have had 26 COPs, they have had decades of blah, blah, blah — and where has that got us?'
 — Greta Thunberg

'I've said as much in the past, we are dealing with a different climate ... I think it's just an obvious fact Australia is getting hard to live in because of these disasters.'
 — Scott Morrison

Mark Knight, *Herald Sun*

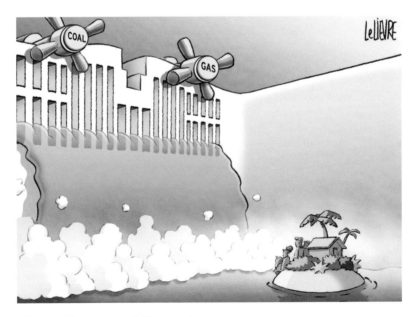

Glen Le Lievre, www.lelievrecartoons.com

Jon Kudelka, *The Saturday Paper*

Glen Le Lievre, www.lelievrecartoons.com

Alan Moir, www.moir.com.au

'We have a rain bomb above south-east Queensland and it continues to come down.'
— Adrian Schrinner, Brisbane lord mayor

'I absolutely understand the frustration, I understand the anger, I understand the disappointment, I understand the sense of abandonment.'
— Scott Morrison

'It's great to be back in Lismore.'
— Bridget McKenzie

'If ... community members hadn't stepped up, then we would have been seeing a death toll in the hundreds of people.'
— Murray Watt

'Climate change will pose more of a threat to vulnerable Australians, such as those with inadequate health care, poor quality housing, and unstable employment.'
— IPCC, March 2022

Matt Golding, *The Sunday Age*

Dean Alston, *The West Australian*

Peter Broelman, www.broelman.com.au

'People are incredibly vulnerable, and it's understandable that they want to express that and the pain that they're going through ... I would be incredibly surprised if people got a happy reception.'
— Barnaby Joyce

'A week is too long to wait for support when your house is inundated with flood water, your animals are at risk, and you have no water, power, food, fuel, or internet.'
— Lismore local

'Why are people having to pitch in and privately hire helicopters when the ADF have access to those resources? They are all questions that need answers.'
— Anthony Albanese

'They're filming themselves, look at them, emptying out a trailer full of rubbish onto the side of a road ... Doing a good job guys. That trailer ain't going to empty itself, is it. Make sure you get it filmed.'
— Lismore local

David Pope, *The Canberra Times*

Jon Kudelka, *The Saturday Paper*

dames, etc.

Reg Lynch, *The Sun Herald*

'We found current systems and reward structures encourage, tolerate, and enable misconduct and processes that are not equipped to prevent or address the consequences of that behaviour.'
— Kate Jenkins

'I was sexually harassed multiple times, sexually assaulted, bullied, and terrorised. And I was told that if I ever sought help or spoke about what happened to me my professional reputation and personal life would be destroyed.'
— Jenkins review participant

'I guess there is a workplace culture of drinking. There's not a lot of accountability. The boys are lads. And that behaviour is celebrated and ... they do treat women, our female staffers and female admin staff, quite differently. Young women, particularly media advisers coming in, particularly the younger women coming in, were like fresh meat and challenges.'
— Jenkins review participant

Cathy Wilcox, *The Sydney Morning Herald*

Fiona Katauskas, *The Echidna*

David Rowe, *The Canberra Times*

'The survival of abuse culture is dependent on submissive smiles and self-defeating surrenders. It is dependent on hypocrisy. My past is only relevant to the extent that I have seen — in fact I have worn — the consequences of civility for the sake of civility.'
— Grace Tame

'I didn't want his sympathy as a father. I wanted him to use his power as prime minister. I wanted him to wield the weight of his office and drive change in the party and our parliament, and out into the country. And one year later, I don't care if the government has improved the way that they talk about these issues. I'm not interested in words any more. I want to see action.'
— Brittany Higgins

'All Anthony would have to do is none of the things that Scott's done.'
— Grace Tame

Peter Broelman, www.broelman.com.au

Jon Kudelka, *The Saturday Paper*

Cathy Wilcox, *The Sydney Morning Herald*

'There is nothing in this bill that seeks to prejudice others, it is a bill that is designed to protect religious expression in this country to ensure that people who have such beliefs are not discriminated against.'
— Scott Morrison

'Concerns have been raised with me that a potential consequence of the amendment is that religious educational institutions will now be able to discriminate against students on the ground of the student's sex, intersex status, or breastfeeding.'
— Michalia Cash

'This bill does not just create a shield from discrimination on the basis of belief, it also creates many swords.'
— Helen Haines

'Why does one group of people have more of a right to be themselves than another, that's what I have to ask the government.'
— Grace Tame

John Farmer, *The Mercury*

Matt Bissett-Johnson, *Rationale Magazine*

Jon Kudelka, *The Saturday Paper*

'I would hope that the prime minister, who has a long history of *wedge-islation*, would focus on doing the right thing by all Australians, not [on] a short-term political manoeuvre.'
 —Graham Perrett

'I felt very much like the woman before Solomon. You will know the story ... two women came and they were arguing over whose child was theirs. And one of their children had died during the night ... And so they go before Solomon and Solomon wisely says, OK, why don't we cut the child in half. And the woman whose child it was said, no, the other woman can have my child. And at that moment, Solomon knew who the mother was ... So, I would rather lay down our attempt to secure those additional protections, than see them compromised or undermined.'
 — Scott Morrison

'The recent unnecessary, hurtful public debate around legal protections for young LGBTIQ+ Australians has had a significant impact on their wellbeing and that of their families and loved ones ... young same-sex attracted people are already five times more likely to attempt suicide — and young transgender Australians are 15 times more likely.'
 — Dan Andrews

Cathy Wilcox,
*The Sydney
Morning Herald*

John Shakespeare,
*The Sydney
Morning Herald*

Mark David, independentaustralia.net

Cathy Wilcox, *The Sydney Morning Herald*

Cathy Wilcox, *The Sydney Morning Herald*

'It's all good, he's got scissors in his hand. He was stabbing me, he was stabbing you.'
  — as reported in Kumanjayi Walker murder trial

'We demand an end to guns in our communities ... this must stop. Do not silence us.'
  — Valerie Napaljarri Martin

'Amongst many unedifying tactics used to unseat me from my preselection victory for Morrison, racial vilification was front and centre and he was directly involved.'
  — Michael Towke

'Scott Morrison told me that, if Michael Towke were to be preselected, there would be a "swing against the Liberal Party in Cook" because of Mr Towke's Lebanese background ... Also during that meeting, Morrison informed me that there was a strong rumour that "Michael Towke is actually a Moslem" [*sic*].'
  — Scott Chapman

blind trust

Cathy Wilcox, *The Sydney Morning Herald*

Jon Kudelka, *The Saturday Paper*

David Pope, *The Canberra Times*

'Ultimately, I decided that if I have to make a choice between seeking to pressure the Trust to break individuals' confidentiality in order to remain in Cabinet, or alternatively forego my Cabinet position, there is only one choice I could, in all conscience, make.'
— Christian Porter

'Australian people need to know who funded this trust, how much they gave, and what they expected to get in return. It is no more acceptable for a member of parliament to keep a donation secret than it is for a minister to keep a donation secret. The Australian people are entitled to know.'
— Mark Dreyfus

'He's had a bad day at the wicket. There's no doubt about that and that issue has been dealt with.'
— Barnaby Joyce

'Perhaps the only certainty now is that there appears no limit to what some will say or allege or do to gain an advantage over a perceived enemy.'
— Christian Porter

Cathy Wilcox, *The Sydney Morning Herald*

'These matters should be looking at criminal conduct, not who your boyfriend is ... The premier of NSW was done over by a bad process, an abuse ... I'm not going to have a kangaroo court in this parliament.'
— Scott Morrison

'This is not the great sort of righteous process — it's a little bit like the Spanish Inquisition.'
— Barnaby Joyce

'To those buffoons who have repeatedly described this commission as a kangaroo court, I would say ... it has a real capacity to undermine the commission's work, and just as importantly, public confidence in public administration.'
— Stephen Rushton

'That's not an ICAC, that's a feather duster.'
— Jacqui Lambie

Alan Moir, www.moir.com.au

John Shakespeare,
*The Sydney
Morning Herald*

Andrew Dyson, *The Age*

'The way in which the government is modelling this proposed commission, it's a disaster. It's worse than having no commission, in my opinion. Picture for yourself what would have happened if the recent banking royal commission had been held in secret. It would have done no good at all. What about the royal commission into institutional child abuse? If that had been conducted in secrecy, it would have been, as it were, an extension of the original problem — the original secrecy.'
— Geoffrey Watson SC

'We can't just hand government over to faceless officials to make decisions that impact the lives of Australians from one end of the country to the other. I actually think there's a great danger in that ... It wouldn't be Australia any more if that was the case, it would be some kind of public autocracy.'
— Scott Morrison

'The reason Scott Morrison doesn't have a national anti-corruption commission is sitting on his front bench.'
— Anthony Albanese

Mark David, independentaustralia.net

Fiona Katauskas, *The Echidna*

Scotty's greatest hits

Warren Brown, *The Daily Telegraph*

Dean Alston, *The West Australian*

Glen Le Lievre, www.lelievrecartoons.com

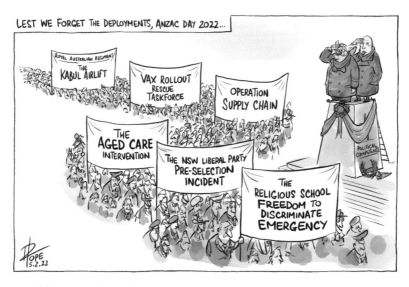

David Pope, *The Canberra Times*

Reg Lynch, *The Sun Herald*

Mark David,
independentaustralia.net

Matt Golding, *The Sunday Age*

Andrew Dyson, *The Age*

Matt Bissett-Johnson, *Melbourne Observer*

'He is a hypocrite and a liar from my observations and that is over a long time. I have never trusted him and I dislike how he earnestly rearranges the truth to a lie.'
— Barnaby Joyce

'Morrison is a horrible, horrible person. He is actively spreading lies and briefing against me.'
— Gladys Berejiklian

'Morrison is about Morrison. Complete psycho. He is desperate and jealous. The mob have worked him out and he is a fraud.'
— government minister, anon

'Their big problem with me, as prime minister, is apparently I go home for Fathers Day, I have a holiday with my family, and I go to church on a Sunday. Get over it, a lot of Australians do.'
— Scott Morrison

'If you don't think there's corruption in Canberra, you're not looking for it. There are more smoking guns on his front bench than in a Clint Eastwood movie.'
— Jason Clare

**First Dog
on the Moon,**
The Guardian

Matt Golding, *The Sunday Age*

'[Scott Morrison] never feels, in himself, insincere or untruthful because he always means exactly what he says; it is just that he means it only in the moment he is saying it. Past and future disappear.'
— Sean Kelly

'Scott has lied to me on many occasions, he has always had a reputation for telling lies.'
— Malcolm Turnbull

'It was like dealing with a two-year-old on a temper tantrum.'
— Jacqui Lambie

'He is adept at running with the foxes and hunting with the hounds, lacking a moral compass and having no conscience … In my public life, I have met ruthless people. Morrison tops the list.'
— Concetta Fierravanti-Wells

Glen Le Lievre, www.lelievrecartoons.com

Jon Kudelka, *The Saturday Paper*

it's not a popularity contest

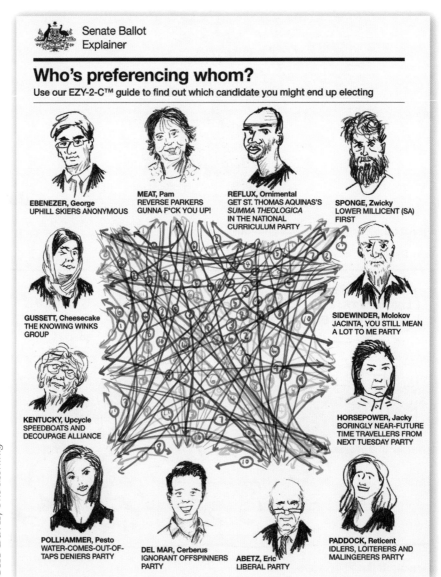

Jon Kudelka, *The Saturday Paper*

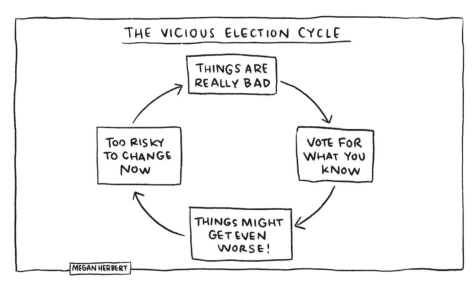

Megan Herbert, *The Age*

Brett Lethbridge, *The Courier Mail*

'It's not a popularity test. You go to the dentist. It doesn't matter if you like him or not, or like her or not. But you want to know that they're good at their job.'
— Scott Morrison

'Who governs matters.'
— Penny Wong

'People are disgruntled. I have people in my ear all the time. They are sick of it. They are sick of all the rorting, sick of pissing money up against the wall. Politics has got worse. People don't like what's happening to our country. There's no accountability, there are no repercussions.'
— Jacqui Lambie

'Australians took Scott Morrison on trust three years ago. They gave him a shot. But they've been disappointed. Worse than that, I think they're angry.'
— Jason Clare

Warren Brown,
The Daily Telegraph

Dean Alston,
The West Australian

Jon Kudelka,
www.kudelka.com.au

Fiona Katauskas, *The Echidna*

John Spooner, *The Australian*

David Rowe, *Australian Financial Review*

'Despite what we have faced, we have remained true to the promise of Australia. And Australia has prevailed. We have kept, as a … government, the promise of Australia.
  — Scott Morrison

'This election is a case of whether voters wish to change the curtains or keep them to avoid the cost, as the current curtains work well, and no-one has proven to us whether the replacements will keep the sun out of our eyes … keep the carpet from fading, and stop other countries from peeking through the windows.'
  — Barnaby Joyce

'I get about the job of seeking to fix and I know sometimes that looks like I'm just pressing on. But you know, as a prime minister, you have to get this stuff done. I will seek to explain my concerns and empathise a lot more. But I tell you what, at the end of the day, what matters most is I get the job done.'
  — Scott Morrison

Matt Golding, *The Sunday Age*

Mark David, independentaustralia.net

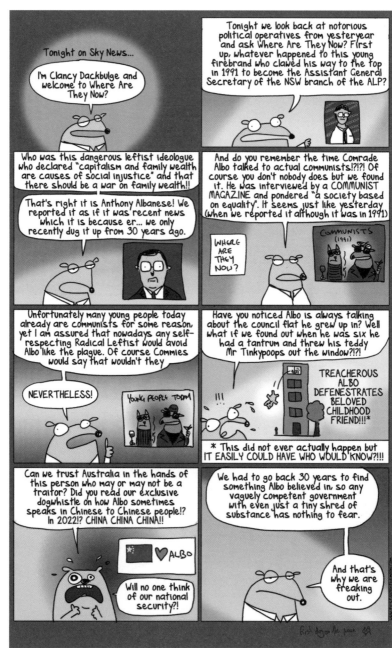

John Spooner, *The Australian*

Matt Bissett-Johnson, *Rationale Magazine*

David Rowe, *Australian Financial Review*

'Anthony Albanese is a loose unit on the economy.'
— Scott Morrison

'Google it, mate … Elections should be about a contest of ideas.'
— Adam Bandt

'From time to time, if ever I make a mistake, I will own it and I will accept responsibility. But, as I quoted the Ramones on day one of the campaign, here is a Taylor Swift comment for you … *Shake it off*.'
— Anthony Albanese

'Sorry. But this is embarrassing for my profession.'
— Laura Tingle

Mark Knight,
Herald Sun

John Shakespeare,
The Sydney Morning Herald

Mark Knight, *Herald Sun*

'I'm looking forward to him re-joining the campaign … He's had a pretty quiet week. I remember when I was in iso I had a very busy week, attending quad summits and doing all those sorts of things.'
 — Scott Morrison

'This is a guy when he was in the Lodge quarantining didn't take his economic policy adviser, he didn't take his national security adviser; he took his photographer.'
 — Anthony Albanese

'I've got a great team, I'm happy to showcase my team every single day.'
 — Scott Morrison

'You see, I know I can count on Penny and Richard, Katie and Jim, and so many others to make the argument for Labor. But who has he got? Alan Tudge and Peter Dutton. The unspeakable and the unthinkable. And then of course, there is Barnaby Joyce, the inexplicable.'
 — Anthony Albanese

Johannes Leak, *The Australian*

Sean Leahy, *The Courier Mail*

David Rowe, *Australian Financial Review*

'Let me assure the people that we entered into an arrangement with China with our eyes wide open, guided by our national interests.'
— Manasseh Sogavare

'I share the same red line that the United States has when it comes to these issues. We won't be having Chinese military naval bases in our region on our doorstep.'
— Scott Morrison

'We don't want our own little Cuba off our coast.'
— Barnaby Joyce

'This is the worst foreign policy blunder in the Pacific that Australia has seen since the end of World War II.'
— Penny Wong

Alan Moir, www.moir.com.au

Peter Broelman, www.broelman.com.au

Brett Lethbridge, *The Courier Mail*

'You shouldn't have to raid your super to buy a home, and you won't under Labor.'
— Jason Clare

'A contender for one of the worst housing policy decisions of the last thirty or so years.'
— Saul Eslake

'I know many people don't like rising interest rates but it's a reflection of the underlying strength of the economy that we can move off these emergency settings.'
— Philip Lowe

'It is not about politics. What happens tomorrow deals with what people pay on their mortgages. That is what I am concerned about. I mean, sometimes you guys always see things through a totally political lens. I don't.'
— Scott Morrison

Dean Alston, *The West Australian*

Christopher Downes, *The Mercury*

Peter Broelman, www.broelman.com.au

'There is a reason why, you know, Anthony Albanese was never given a financial portfolio by ... by any of Labor leaders in the past. It is because they knew he couldn't be trusted with money.'
— Scott Morrison

'What we're talking about here is people on minimum wages. It's $20.33 an hour ... if the Fair Work Commission grants a 5 per cent increase, that's two cups of coffee a day.'
— Anthony Albanese

'If Mr Albanese thinks small businesses around the country can have a 5 per cent increase in their wages bill on top of all the other things they're facing ... people won't be worrying about what their wages are, they will be worrying about whether they have a job.'
— Scott Morrison

'You deserve more than thanks. You deserve a government that cares about secure work.'
— Anthony Albanese

Dean Alston, *The West Australian*

Johannes Leak, *The Australian*

Glen Le Lievre, www.lelievrecartoons.com

'Australians know that I can be a bit of a bulldozer when it comes to issues and I suspect you guys know that too ... I know there are things that are going to have to change with the way I do things.'
— Scott Morrison

'A bulldozer wrecks things. A bulldozer knocks things over. I'm a builder ... The prime minister is putting his hand up and saying, "I'll change". Well, if you want change, change the government on 21 May.'
— Anthony Albanese

'Morrison became the first leader in more than 50 years to spurn [the National Press Club]. Crash tackling a little boy on a footy field was obviously a much better use of his time. A strange unit for sure.'
— Niki Savva

'Australians have conflict fatigue. They want solutions, not arguments.'
— Anthony Albanese

John Farmer, *The Mercury*

Sean Leahy, *The Courier Mail*

Matt Golding, *The Sunday Age*

'We spent a full fucking week being transphobes in parliament and then we spent weeks during the campaign doing the exact same thing, and it was fucking insane ... The transphobe thing was an absolute disaster. We clearly didn't have enough economic policies.'
— Liberal MP, anon

'A cynical person would say Deves was put up to murder the moderates. They were totally kneecapped by that ... Barely able to do any media at all because that's all they were going to be asked about.'
— Liberal MP, anon

'Morrison was the kind of clever who believes his genius can never be decoded by someone else ... Sometimes, that is indistinguishable from the madness of kings. And in his case, Morrison believed his infallibility until the very end. His office enabled it, they briefed it, and they injected it into the campaign at every opportunity.'
— Liberal MP, anon

Cathy Wilcox, *The Sydney Morning Herald*

Megan Herbert, *The Age*

Cathy Wilcox, *The Sydney Morning Herald*

'So-called independents are subverting democracy. Zoe Daniel is getting secret money from Climate 200.'
— Tim Wilson

'More than 2000 volunteers, walking the streets of Kooyong every day in the teal T-shirts. That's the wave that's going to carry me to Canberra.'
— Monique Ryan

'They're decapitating the moderate section of the Liberal Party, and the fruits of their labour will be ashes in their mouth because you're going to have a movement of the Liberal Party to the right if they succeed.'
— Barnaby Joyce

'We've had the exemplary role models of Cathy McGowan, Helen Haines, Zali Steggall — they're not wreckers, they're builders. You don't read about their antics, you read about their politics.'
— Simon Holmes à Court

John Spooner, *The Australian*

Johannes Leak, *The Australian*

David Rowe, *Australian Financial Review*

'Why would you do this job if you don't want to leave a legacy and change Australia for the better?'
— Anthony Albanese

'The Albo I know is a man of courage and conviction. The most steadfast of friends. The toughest of fighters. And the kindest of hearts. I know no-one braver for his cause. No-one more reliable when you need him. He will stand with you when it is easy and when it is hard. Because he is driven by belief and compassion and integrity.'
— Penny Wong

'I said I've been underestimated my whole life ... I have also been lifted up by others who saw something in me and who encouraged me in life on this journey. And I pledge to the Australian people here tonight, I am here not to occupy the space, but to make a positive difference each and every day.
— Anthony Albanese

Matt Golding, *The Sunday Age*

Jon Kudelka, *The Saturday Paper*

that's not my job

Matt Bissett-Johnson, *Melbourne Observer*

Warren Brown, *The Daily Telegraph*

Matt Golding, *The Sunday Age*

'The Liberal Party's experiment with the poison of leftism and progressivism must be over.'
 — Alex Antic

'He fucked us and his fingerprints are absolutely fuckin' everywhere on that. The bloke thinks he is a master strategist. He is a fuckwit.'
 — Liberal MP, anon

'When the Liberal Party goes too far to the right, we lose in the centre.'
 — Matt Kean

'The absence of a program for the future ... of some kind of manifesto, hurt us very badly ... There's a shelf-life to arguing that we can manage things better ... you have got to keep arguing for something.'
 — John Howard

'I think it took people three years to realise what a horrible person he is.'
 — Liberal MP, anon

David Rowe, *Australian Financial Review*

'I hope now, in moving from such tough portfolios, the Australian public can see the rest of my character.'
 — Peter Dutton

'I believe passionately in the National Party ... we are the conscience of rural and regional Australia.'
 — David Littleproud

'We know that we didn't receive the support of all women at the last election and my message to the women of Australia is: we hear you.'
 — Sussan Ley

'I suppose you think I am sad. Not really.'
 — Barnaby Joyce

Mark Knight, *Herald Sun*

Brett Lethbridge, *The Courier Mail*

David Rowe, *Australian Financial Review*

'I've got a much better relationship with Peter Dutton than Scott Morrison. Peter Dutton has never broken a confidence I've had with him.'
 — Anthony Albanese

'I'm not as bad as the ABC might sometimes report.'
 — Peter Dutton

'I think there will be a lot of children who have watched a lot of Harry Potter films who will be very frightened of what they are seeing on TV at night, that's for sure.'
 — Tanya Plibersek

'We won't be Labor lite.'
 — Peter Dutton

Peter Broelman, www.broelman.com.au

Jon Kudelka, *The Saturday Paper*

Glen Le Lievre, www.lelievrecartoons.com

'Do you believe that if you lose an election that God still loves you and has a plan for you? I do. I still believe in miracles. God has secured your future, all of it. Yeah, even that bit.'
— Scott Morrison

'I'm not going to slice up some kiwi fruit with passionfruit onto a cowpat and tell you it's a chocolate pavlova ... The dream that is Australia is too important to leave to the window-lickers in the Labor Party and the Greens.'
— James McGrath

'We don't trust in governments, we don't trust in United Nations, thank goodness ... But as someone who's been in it, if you are putting your faith in those things, like I put my faith in the Lord, you are making a mistake. They're earthly, they are fallible. I'm so glad we have a bigger hope.'
— Scott Morrison

First Dog
on the
Moon,
The Guardian

Glen Le Lievre, www.lelievrecartoons.com

'I, as prime minister, was responsible pretty much for every single thing that was going on.'
— Scott Morrison

'Australians knew during the election campaign that I was running a shadow ministry. What they didn't know was that Scott Morrison was running a shadow government.'
— Anthony Albanese

'I'm astonished that Mr Morrison thought he could do it, astonished that prime minister and Cabinet went along with it. I'm even more astonished that the governor-general was party to it. This is sinister stuff.'
— Malcolm Turnbull

'I am going to ask him to resign and leave parliament.'
— Karen Andrews

Mark Knight, *Herald Sun*

Alan Moir, www.moir.com.au

bon appetit, Jim ...

Fiona Katauskas, *The Echidna*

Mark Knight, *Herald Sun*

David Rowe, *Australian Financial Review*

'We can't do everything that we would like to do ... If we don't do something about improving the fiscal position of the budget, the impact on households will just flow on down the track ... we do have a few decisions to make and we make them with what we've been dealt with ... $1 trillion of debt.'
   — Anthony Albanese

'Partly it's the nature of the beast. And then you have times like this when the breadth and scale of what has been left in the bottom drawer is negligent in the extreme.'
   — incoming Labor minister

'The economic picture I have set out today represents a convergence of challenges, the kind of which comes around once in a generation ... But this once-in-a-generation challenge also represents a once-in-a-generation opportunity for our country. The opportunity to build a better future.'
   — Jim Chalmers

First Dog on the Moon, *The Guardian*

Alan Moir, www.moir.com.au

Andrew Weldon, *The Big Issue*

John Spooner, *The Australian*

'The budget we inherited is bursting with waste and rorts, booby-trapped by expiring measures, and burdened by long-term demographic challenges that come with critical and necessary spending.'
  — Jim Chalmers

'While wage growth clearly has not been the driving force of recent increases in Australian inflation, or indeed inflation around the world, the continuing impact of COVID and the sharp increase in global energy prices associated with Russia's invasion of Ukraine clearly have.'
  — Australia Institute

'Australians are paying a hefty price for a wasted decade. They know their new government didn't make this mess, but we take responsibility for cleaning it up.'
  — Jim Chalmers

'We're not suggesting that Labor can change those global circumstances ... but they can put the national interest first, ahead of pet projects, ahead of ideological fixations, and ahead of vested interests.'
  — Angus Taylor

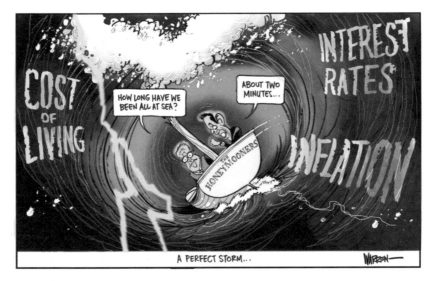

Warren Brown, *The Daily Telegraph*

Cathy Wilcox, *The Sydney Morning Herald*

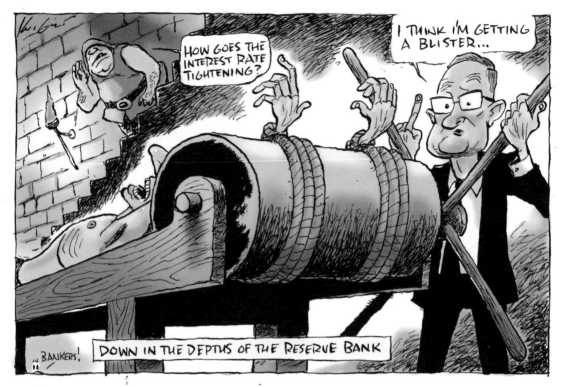

Mark Knight, *Herald Sun*

'The harsh truth is that households won't feel the benefits of higher wages while inflation eats up these wage increases, and then some. Real wages growth relies on moderating inflation and getting wages moving again.'
— Jim Chalmers

'If we don't have higher interest rates, then we're going to have higher inflation persist, eventually that will have to be addressed and we know how from history that's addressed. It's addressed through much higher interest rates ... and a sharp slowing in the economy.'
— Philip Lowe

'Australia isn't experiencing a wage-price spiral, it's at the beginning of a price-profit spiral. The national accounts show it is rising profits, not rising costs, that are driving Australia's inflation. While workers are being asked to make sacrifices in the name of controlling inflation, the data makes clear that it is the corporate sector that needs to tighten its belt.'
— Richard Denniss

Warren Brown, *The Daily Telegraph*

Christopher Downes, *The Mercury*

David Pope, *The Canberra Times*

'One of the things that people have a right to believe is that when a politician makes a commitment before an election, they keep it, and I intend to do that.'
— Anthony Albanese

'If even one thing — one prediction, one assumption — does not materialise in the way the budget hopes, they are in trouble. Even if things hold up, the last stage of tax cuts can only be funded by budget cuts.'
— Jim Chalmers, 2019

'The federal Labor government plans on spending $22 billion over 10 years on the stage 3 tax cuts, but only $10 billion on building social and affordable housing, which is a real kick in the teeth for the hundreds of thousands of people in desperate need of a home.'
— Max Chandler-Mather

'We are worried that Labor won't have the guts to do what's necessary.'
— Adam Bandt

Jon Kudelka, *The Saturday Paper*

Andrew Dyson, *The Age*

Cathy Wilcox, *The Sydney Morning Herald*

'I am now more convinced than ever that Australians crave leadership that is inclusive and collaborative and that puts the public interest first. That's not to say that passionately arguing your case can't be constructive. It is sometimes essential. The problem is when the argument becomes the end in itself.'
— Anthony Albanese

'The Australian flag does not represent me or my people. It represents the colonisation of these lands.'
— Lidia Thorpe

'You have a lot of experience, some nasty people would say devious cunning, you develop over a period of almost 50 years. I will most certainly be using every centile of that devious cunning.'
— Bob Katter

'I want to see a parliament that functions much better than the last one. One where there's genuine debate and dialogue and discussion.
— Anthony Albanese

David Pope, *The Canberra Times*

Johannes Leak, *The Australian*

Matt Golding, *The Sunday Age*

'There's no end to the list of worthy, important things we could be spending the money on in the health portfolio, but there is an end to the money ... The Australian community understands, and indeed wants, the country to move to a new phase in confronting this pandemic.'
— Mark Butler

'I want to make sure that people aren't left behind, that vulnerable people are looked after, and that no-one is faced with the unenviable choice of not being able to isolate properly without losing an income.'
— Anthony Albanese

'Albanese needs to apologise to every casual worker who suffered stress as a result of this flip-flopping.'
— Sussan Ley

'COVID is one of the biggest issues the country faces at the moment, but the country doesn't know it.'
— Brendan Crabb, Burnet Institute

Christopher Downes, *The Mercury*

Fiona Katauskas, *The Echidna*

ideally, you wouldn't start from here

David Pope,
The Canberra Times

Andrew Dyson,
The Age

Andrew Weldon, *The Big Issue*

'If Europe went into a broader war and there was a severe economic downturn, would the government want to have a legislated 43 per cent? Or would they want to adjust and deal with the reality of the times?'
— Peter Dutton

'If you're going to legislate targets then they should be Dutton-proof.'
— Adam Bandt

'Nuclear energy is a mature, proven technology; it can provide the reliable, emissions-free, base-load electricity Australia needs.'
— Peter Dutton

'They seem obsessed by nuclear reactors. They're ignoring the future. They are stuck in the past. They're frozen in time while the world warms around them. We will not be held hostage to that behaviour.'
— Anthony Albanese

Mark Knight, *Herald Sun*

'The Albanese government will do whatever is needed to make sure Australians have ongoing access to the gas and energy sources that belong to the people of Australia.'
— Madeleine King

'LNG exporters have diverted most of their excess gas to overseas spot markets, with as much as 70 per cent of the excess volume going overseas in recent years.'
— ACCC

'If Australia today said we are not going to export any more coal, you would see ... a significant loss to our economy [and] a replacement with coal from other countries that's likely to produce higher emissions because of the quality of our product.'
— Anthony Albanese

'The new government is already sounding far too much like the old government.'
— Adam Bandt

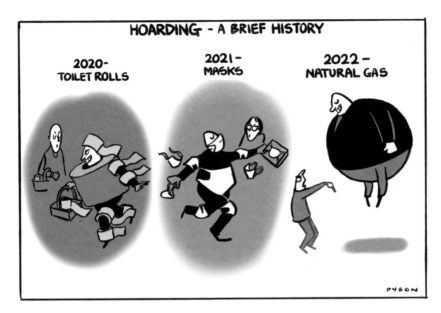

Andrew Dyson, *The Age*

John Spooner, *The Australian*

Peter Broelman, www.broelman.com.au

'We have to be very clear: 43 per cent is a political target, it is not a scientific target.'
— Zali Steggall

'We have to actually bank some of these gains and I want to see a target with integrity ... as a floor, not a ceiling, and then ramping up ambition over time.'
— David Pocock

'People want politicians to work together on something as important as climate ... but Labor's *my way or the highway* approach is the kind of hairy-chested politics the public has just rejected.'
— Adam Bandt

'The broader the base of political consensus around this bill, the easier the case for the major clean economy investments Australia needs in manufacturing, energy, resources, and more.'
— Innes Willox

Fiona Katauskas, *The Echidna*

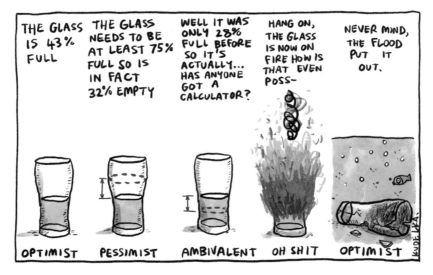

Jon Kudelka, *The Saturday Paper*

David Rowe, *Australian Financial Review*

'It's a good day for Australia. It's a good day for our economy. It's a good day for our future. The climate wars may or may not be over, but they're certainly in retreat.'
— Chris Bowen

'Our preference was to improve and pass the bill. In this parliament, where less than a third of the country voted Labor, Labor has some mandate and the Greens have some mandate. But more important is our mandate from the planet and the laws of physics. If Labor continues to open up new coal and gas, the planet will burn, and that is the mandate that we all need to listen to.'
— Adam Bandt

'If the Greens party haven't learned from what they did in 2009 — that was something that led to a decade of inaction and delay and denial — then that will be a matter for them.'
— Anthony Albanese

Alan Moir, www.moir.com.au

Glen Le Lievre, www.lelievrecartoons.com

David Rowe, *Australian Financial Review*

'The parliament functioned effectively to support the mandate that we received at the election, with the exception of the Coalition, who continue to be stuck in time while the world warms around it.'
— Anthony Albanese

'The climate wars are nearly over.'
— Zali Steggall

'This is just the end of the beginning in our action on climate change.'
— Monique Ryan

'This is round one. Over the next six months, the battle will be fought on a number of fronts.'
— Adam Bandt

David Pope, *The Canberra Times*

Matt Golding, *The Sunday Age*

David Rowe, *Australian Financial Review*

'In a rapidly changing climate, with declining biodiversity, the general outlook for our environment is deteriorating. The impacts of this will affect us all. It is in our own interest to understand, protect, and restore the health of our environment ... It is also our responsibility. Our environment has intrinsic value beyond direct human use.'
— State of the Environment report

'Years of warnings that were ignored or kept secret. Promises made, but not delivered. Dodgy behaviour, undermining public confidence. Brutal funding cuts. Wilful neglect ... It's time to change that.'
— Tanya Plibersek

'Environment minister Sussan Ley showed a callous disregard for threatened species — including our own ... Tanya Plibersek has to address these issues as a matter of urgency.'
— Monique Ryan

Fiona Katauskas, *The Echidna*

David Pope, *The Canberra Times*

Badiucao, *The Age*

'I believe there is room in Australian hearts, for the Statement from the Heart ... We are seeking a momentous change — but it is also a very simple one.'
— Anthony Albanese

'All arguments against the Voice are based on the concept that we're a race of people and that no race should have more recognition than another. That is complete furphy. We're not a race — we're over 600 cultural groups ... we're the peoples of this land. We ask for decency, a rightful place in the nation.'
— Marcia Langton

'I've had my fill of being symbolically recognised ... I've had enough of it. It's really nothing to improve the lives of marginalised people ... We don't want to see all these symbolic gestures, we want to see real action. We want to see change for the benefit of not just marginalised Australians but all Australians.'
— Jacinta Price

Cathy Wilcox, *The Sydney Morning Herald*

Johannes Leak, *The Australian*

a new dawn

Alan Moir, www.moir.com.au

Cathy Wilcox, *The Sydney Morning Herald*

David Pope, *The Canberra Times*

'The Assange case is unique ... The US is seeking to establish a precedent where it could seek to extradite any journalist anywhere in the world for disclosure of US information.'
— Greg Barns

'I've said for some time that enough is enough ... He has paid a big price for the publication of that information already and I do not see what purpose is served by the ongoing pursuit of Mr Assange.'
— Anthony Albanese

'The very manner in which the government has sought to conduct the prosecution [of Bertnard Collaery] appears to me to be an affront to the rule of law.'
— Mark Dreyfus

'The Australian government is the real villain in this case, having made the appalling decision to spy on East Timor, which is one of the poorest countries in south-east Asia.'
— Andrew Wilkie

David Pope, *The Canberra Times*

'By supporting peace and sovereignty in Europe, we are underscoring our iron-clad commitment to these norms in our own region, the Indo-Pacific.'
— Anthony Albanese

'We are disappointed by the fact that China has not been able to condemn the Russian invasion of Ukraine, that China is spreading many of the false narratives about NATO, the West, and also that China and Russia are more close now than they have ever been before.'
— Jens Stoltenberg, NATO

'They should also stop trying to launch a new Cold War. What they should do is give up their Cold War mindset, zero-sum games, and stop doing things that create enemies.'
— Zhao Lijian

'We always think about the future, not the past. [Albanese's] not responsible for what happened.'
— Emmanuel Macron

Glen Le Lievre, www.lelievrecartoons.com

Glen Le Lievre, www.lelievrecartoons.com

David Rowe, *Australian Financial Review*

'Your visit to Fiji ... your first bilateral visit, represents a very strong shift in Australia's regional outlook.'
— Henry Puna, Forum Secretary-General

'China has made its intentions clear [but] so too are the intentions of the new Australian government. We want to help build a stronger Pacific family.'
— Anthony Albanese

'It is not in someone's interest, nor the interest of the region for any military base, to be established in any Pacific island ... the moment we establish a foreign military base, we immediately become an enemy.'
— Manasseh Sogavare

'I know the imperative we all share to take serious action to reduce emissions and transform our economies. Nothing is more central to the security and economies of the Pacific.'
— Penny Wong

Fiona Katauskas, *The Echidna*

Johannes Leak, *The Australian*

David Pope, *The Canberra Times*

'You got sworn in, you got on a plane and if you fall asleep while you're here, it's OK. I don't know how you're doing it!'
— Joe Biden

'We have had a change of government in Australia, but Australia's commitment to the Quad has not changed and will not change.'
— Anthony Albanese

'We want to take this in a very sober and deliberate manner. We don't underestimate the difficulties we've had in our bilateral relationship.'
— Richard Marles

'The root cause of the difficulties in Chinese and Australian relations in recent years lies in the insistence of previous Australian governments to treat China as an "opponent" and even a "threat".'
— Wang Yi

John Spooner, *The Australian*

Badiucao, @badiucao

John Spooner, *The Australian*

'We live in a time where the region is being reshaped, and what is important is that countries work together to ensure that region remains peaceful, prosperous, and respectful of sovereignty.'
— Penny Wong

'We are linked not just by geography, we are linked by choice ... It will be by working with Indonesia that we most effectively tackle the many challenges we face.'
— Anthony Albanese

'It is the region where I am from. Having spent my early years in Kota Kinabalu, I look forward to the great honour of returning to the city as Australia's foreign minister.'
— Penny Wong

'It's important that constituents know that people are on the job and we hadn't heard from Mr Albanese for 48 hours.'
— Angus Taylor

Peter Broelman, www.broelman.com.au

Peter Broelman, www.broelman.com.au

Cathy Wilcox, *The Sydney Morning Herald*

'Facing deliberately heightened military threats, Taiwan will not back down. We will firmly uphold our nation's sovereignty and continue to hold the line of defence for democracy.'
— President Tsai Ing-wen

'These moves, like playing with fire, are extremely dangerous. Those who play with fire will perish by it.'
— Chinese Foreign Affairs Ministry

'All parties should consider how they best contribute to de-escalating the current tensions and we all want peace and stability in the Taiwan Strait.'
— Penny Wong

'Today the world faces a choice between democracy and autocracy. America's determination to preserve democracy, here in Taiwan and around the world, remains ironclad.'
— Nancy Pelosi

David Rowe, *Australian Financial Review*

'We are at the edge of war with Russia and China on issues which we partly created, without any concept of how this is going to end or what it's supposed to lead to.'
  —Henry Kissinger

Badiucao, *The Age*

'We reserve the option of taking all necessary measures ... As to what is the meaning of *all necessary means* — you can use your imagination.'
— Xiao Qian, Chinese ambassador

'My personal understanding is that once Chinese Taiwan comes back to the motherland, there might be a process for the people of Taiwan to have a correct understanding of China.'
— Xiao Qian, Chinese ambassador

'It's absolutely imperative we review the current strategic circumstances, which I rate the worst I have ever seen in my career and lifetime.'
— Angus Houston

'We are in what I describe as the decade of living dangerously.'
— Kevin Rudd

Jim Pavlidis, *The Age*

Johannes Leak, *The Australian*

the state of the union

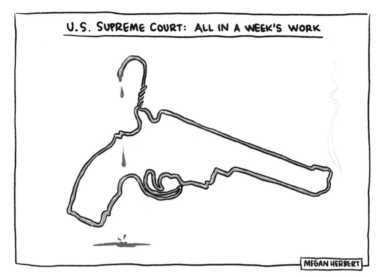

Megan Herbert, *The Age*

David Pope, *The Canberra Times*

Cathy Wilcox, *The Sydney Morning Herald*

'Young women today will come of age with fewer rights than their mothers and grandmothers.'
— dissenting opinion, US Supreme Court

'Calls into question other rights that we thought were settled, such as the right to use birth control, the right to same-sex marriage, the right to interracial marriage.'
— Kamala Harris, vice-president

'This opinion reflects the fact that a radical faction of the Supreme Court is moving in a maximalist direction.'
— Prof. Paul Schiff Berman

'Our great nation now teeters on the brink of a widening abyss.'
— Jimmy Carter

David Rowe, *Australian Financial Review*

'All I'm asking you to do is just say it was corrupt and leave the rest to me.'
— Donald Trump to Department of Justice

'He lied, he bullied, he betrayed his oath. He tried to destroy our democratic institutions.'
— Bennie Thompson, January 6 committee

'In our nation's 246-year history, there has never been an individual who is a greater threat to our republic than Donald Trump.'
— Dick Cheney

'My beautiful home ... is currently under siege, raided, and occupied by a large group of FBI agents.'
— Donald Trump

Matt Golding, *The Sunday Age*

Christopher Downes, *The Mercury*

David Pope, *The Canberra Times*

'I also want to thank ... my friend, Boris Johnson. You got Brexit done, you crushed Jeremy Corbyn, you rolled out the vaccine and you stood up to Vladimir Putin. You were admired from Kyiv to Carlisle.'
— Liz Truss

In my lifetime I have never seen a PM coming in with lower political capital.'
— cabinet minister, anon

'That impulse to do her duty carried her right through into her tenth decade to the very moment in Balmoral ... when she saw off her fourteenth prime minister, and welcomed her fifteenth.'
— Boris Johnson

'Through the noise and turbulence of the years, she embodied and exhibited a timeless decency and an enduring calm. This time of mourning will pass, but the deep respect and warm regard in which Australians have always held for her will never fade. May she rest in eternal peace.'
— Anthony Albanese

David Pope, *The Canberra Times*

Matt Golding, *The Sunday Age*

Fiona Katauskas, *The Echidna*

'I say to everyone here, all of my parliamentary colleagues, don't miss the chance, because you're not here for that long ... And when you're sitting on the porch, thinking about what you did, you can either have a source of pride, or a source of regret. There's no middle path ... Make it a source of pride.'
— Anthony Albanese